GW00738149

THE WAY OF THE JEWS

ISBN 0 7175 0875 7

First Published by 1972
by
HULTON EDUCATIONAL PUBLICATIONS LTD
Raans Road, Amersham, Bucks.

Reprinted 1975
Second Edition 1980
Reprinted 1985

Printed in Hong Kong by Wing King Tong Ltd.

THE WAY
OF THE
JEWS

by

Rabbi Dr. LOUIS JACOBS

illustrated by

EDWARD MORTELMANS

SECOND EDITION

HULTON EDUCATIONAL PUBLICATIONS

CONTENTS

6

Moses

The Jews

Judaism is the religion of the Jews. It differs from most other religions in having as its hero not a single great person but a whole people. Judaism knows, too, of great men such as Abraham, the founder of the Jewish people who lived about 4,000 years ago, Moses, King David and so on. But while it is impossible to think of Christianity without Jesus, of Buddhism without Buddha, of Islam without Mohammed, it is quite possible to think of Judaism as existing without Abraham or Moses or David. The ideal of Judaism is that of a whole people doing what God wants them to do, which is to be just and kind and to worship Him. There have been outstanding men among the Jews but, as Judaism sees it, these do not count more in the eyes of God than the ordinary good Jew who carries out his duties faithfully and well. There are about 14 million Jews in the world today. Two and a half million Jews live in the State of Israel; five million in the United States of America; three million in Soviet Russia and the rest in many other countries. In Great Britain there are around half a million Jews, a half of them living in London. For all the differences in language and dress the main features of Jewish life are the same in every part of the world. A Jew from New York who visited

A Synagogue

London or Shanghai or Jerusalem would feel at home among the Jews there. He would find the same pattern of religious life that he knew in the place where he was born.

The Synagogue

Jews worship God in the synagogue and the language in which they recite their prayers is Hebrew. Hebrew is the language in which the greater part of the Bible is written because it was the language used in Palestine

10

by the ancestors of the Jewish people. The letters are shaped quite differently from those of the European languages and Hebrew is read from right to left. The actual word "synagogue" is not Hebrew but comes from the Greek word meaning a "gathering". The meaning is a gathering of people who come together to worship God and the name is given to the building in which they are gathered. There are no rules as to how a synagogue should be built. Some synagogues are very splendid affairs with marble pillars, huge stained glass windows and costly fabrics. Others are quite simple structures, four walls and a few benches. Indeed any room, even a room in a private house, can serve as a synagogue if people choose to worship there.

The central place in the synagogue is in the east and is a kind of built-in cupboard with a curtain across it. This is known as the "ark". In the ark are scrolls made of parchment on which are written by hand the Five Books of Moses, the first five books of the Bible. The scrolls are beautifully written. It takes a good deal of training to produce a skilful scribe who is able to write a scroll. Skilful though he is, it generally takes him about a year to complete a single scroll. He uses a special dark ink, the secret of whose manufacture is handed down from one scribe to the other. The scrolls are wrapped round with mantles of fine material and are decorated with bells and other ornaments of gold or silver.

11

The ark containing the scrolls

On the great festivals of the Jewish year and at certain other times the scrolls are removed from the ark and taken in procession around the synagogue, the bells tinkling as they are moved. A portion of a scroll is then read aloud so that the congregation can hear the Biblical teachings and follow them in their lives.

The worshippers in the synagogue wear shawls made of wool or silk with tassels at the four corners. The tassels are to remind them that they must never forget God's law, rather as we sometimes tie a knot in our handkerchief if we want to remind ourselves of something we do not wish to forget. There are no special priests in the synagogue. The services can be conducted by anyone who knows enough Hebrew and whose voice is good enough to sing properly the melodies to which the prayers are recited. This is because, as we have seen, Judaism does not like to single out any one person or group of persons. All the people are priests. There is a Rabbi (the word simply means "teacher") but he is not a priest. His job is to teach the Torah (a word we shall now examine) to his congregation.

A Rabbi

13

The Torah

The word Torah, one of the key words in Judaism, means "teaching". It means first of all the Bible but it includes, too, all the teachings of Judaism. All the explanations of the Bible and all the new ideas of the Jewish scholars throughout the ages are called the Torah. Judaism believes that one of the most precious gifts God has given to man is his brain. Man is a being who thinks about life. That is why Judaism has always had respect for those who use their minds to think and that is why the Jew is expected to study the Torah. This study of the Torah is never ending. There is so much to learn and so little time in which to do it. Jewish children, for instance, begin to learn Hebrew — and this is by no means easy — at an early age so that they can read the teachings of the Torah in the language in which they were written, as well as recite and understand the Hebrew prayers. But it does not stop there. For the whole of the Jew's life he is expected to set aside some time in which he studies the Torah. It is not wealth or power or fame that win a Jew respect among his fellow-Jews. The greatest respect is only paid to those who are learned in the Torah and the more a man knows of the Torah the more he is admired. In former times no Jew could hold any office in the Jewish community unless
14

he was a learned man. It is still the fondest hope of Jewish parents to have children who know the Torah.

The Torah

The History

In the book of Genesis (the first book of the Bible) it is told how Abraham, the son of an idolater, was ordered by God to leave his father's house and the land in which he was born to journey towards a land which, God said, He would show him. This means that Abraham made a complete break with the practice of his time for men to worship strange gods, idols of gold, silver and wood. Abraham came to see that these gods are nothing and that those who worship them are fools. There is only one God and He made everything that there is. It was a very hard thing, to do what Abraham did, to say that all men of his day were mistaken and that only God, and not the idols, is real. The land in which Abraham settled was Palestine. Here he lived with his family and here, too, lived his son Isaac and his son Jacob and their families. Jacob was also known as Israel and so the Bible calls the children of Jacob and the people which were descended from them "the children of Israel" or the Israelites, the ancient name for the Jewish people. (The word "Jew" is a later word, from Judah, one of Jacob's sons.)

Jacob's family went down to Egypt where eventually the Israelites were made slaves by the Pharaoh, the king of Egypt. Here they were forced to build structures like the pyramids still to be seen in Egypt. Moses, the great leader, adopted by Pharaoh's daughter, came to see how bad slavery was. It was not right, he felt deeply in his heart, for some men to force others to work for them without their having any choice in the matter. He came to feel that God had sent him to lead the unfortunate slaves out of Egypt. This he eventually succeeded in doing and the Israelites came back to Palestine to live a life of freedom.

The baby Moses

Soon after the Israelites had left Egypt, the tradition tells, they came to Mount Sinai where God called Moses onto the mountain and there gave him the teachings for his people, especially the Ten Commandments, of which more will be said soon. Moses himself did not live to see his people enter Palestine but a number of men arose to succeed Moses and to lead the people there. Among these were the Hebrew prophets, men like Isaiah, Amos, Hosea and Jeremiah whose works are now part of the Bible.

The prophets taught the people in the name of God to behave righteously, not to oppress one another, to help the poor, to hate warfare and violence, and, of course, to worship the one God and not go after the idols. The people did not always listen to the prophets. This brought about their downfall for unless a people behaves justly its policies are bound to fail. The king of Babylon, with the strange name of Nebuchadnezzer, captured the land and took many of its people captive into Babylon. But after seventy years, under the direction of the Persian king Cyrus, who was now the ruler of Babylon, some of the people returned to rebuild the Temple, the house in Jerusalem where the Jews gathered for the worship of God. The Temple was a magnificent building. If you go to Jerusalem today you can still see part of the Western Wall of the Temple which has stood there for over two thousand years.

18

The Western Wall of the Temple in Jerusalem

Almost two thousand years ago the Romans destroyed the Temple and the Jews were scattered all over the world. But they kept alive the dream that one day they would return to Palestine. In this century the ancient dream came true. The Jewish people founded the State of Israel which has now been in existence for over twenty-five years.

19

The Teachings

Here are some of the main teachings of Judaism. In the Five Books of Moses we read: "Hear O Israel! The Lord our God the Lord is One. And thou shalt love the Lord thy God with all thy heart and with all thy soul and with all thy might". There, too, we read another famous rule: "Thou shalt love thy neighbour as thyself".

The Ten Commandments are ten rules of conduct by which man is expected to live. Although the one concerning the Sabbath is directed to Jews alone, the rest of the ten are sound rules for all men and, indeed, they have been a mighty force for righteousness for many many millions of human beings. The Ten Commandments are:

1. There is only one God.
2. No other gods or idols must be worshipped.
3. God's name must be respected.
4. The sabbath day must be kept as a holy day.
5. Honour must be given to parents.
6. Men must not commit murder.
7. A man must not take another man's wife away from him.
8. Men must not steal from one another.

9. Men must not give false witness against one another.
10. Men must not plan to get hold for themselves of that which belongs to others.

One of the prophets replied to the question what it is that God wants man to do: "Only be just, love mercy and walk humbly with God". The prophets dreamed of the day when war will be banished from human society when, as they put it, men will "beat their swords into ploughing instruments and their spears into pruning-forks, nation will not lift up sword against nation, neither will they learn war any more". This means that one day men will learn to use the talents God has given them for the betterment of mankind not for destruction. The prophets dreamed, too, of the day when all men will recognise God and serve Him.

Family life, Judaism teaches, is God's will for mankind. People should marry and have children and live in harmony together. Parents must care for their children, seeing to it that they are well clothed and fed, attending to their education and training them to lead good and useful lives. Children, in turn, must respect their parents and look after them in their old age. Old people generally are to be treated with respect. Whenever an old man or woman or a scholar enters a room the people present are expected to rise to their feet to show them honour. One of the leading Rabbis in ancient times was asked: "What is Judaism?" and he was asked to give such a short answer that he could give it while he stood on one leg. His reply was: "That which is hateful to you do not do unto your neighbour. This is the whole of the Torah. All the rest is explanation. Now go and learn more about it".

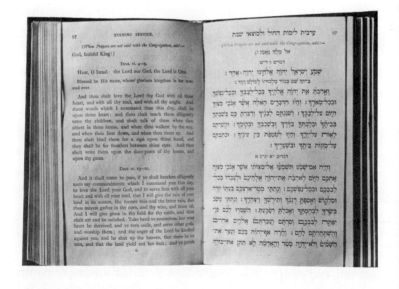

A Jewish 'prayer book'

Good Deeds

Doing "good deeds" is particularly stressed in Judaism. It is no use at all learning all about high ideals unless one is prepared to practise them in daily living. So Judaism urges men to be honest in all their dealings. They must fix only fair prices for the goods they sell. Such goods must not be dressed up to look better than they really are and so fool the customer. Cheating of any kind is strictly forbidden. To deprive a man of his livelihood is one of the worst sins. Men must speak gently to one another. It is forbidden to give others misleading advice, to tell them that something is good for them when really it is the opposite. To put another person to shame in public is compared by the Rabbis to the crime of murder. These ancient Rabbis also say that a man is never closer to God than when he shows compassion to those who suffer. He must, therefore, visit the sick and comfort those who mourn, he must give food to the hungry and garments to those who have few of their own. In Jewish communities everywhere there are special societies whose aim it is to collect money for the needs of the poor.

The highest degree of charity, a Rabbi taught eight hundred years ago, is to help quietly a man whose business is going down so that he is saved from be-

24 The rich placed sums of money in the chest for the poor

coming poor. A man should always give charity in secret. We are told that in the Temple there was a large chest into which the rich would place sums of money. When the money was later distributed to the poor they would have no idea to whom they were grateful and would therefore feel no embarrassment.

Employers are obliged to treat their workers well. They must pay them proper wages and give them sufficient time off. Workers have a right to strike. But workers, too, must put in a good day's work and not take advantage of the man who employs them. Manual labour is in no way disgraceful. Indeed, some of the greatest of the ancient Jewish teachers earned their living by working with their hands, as shoemakers, woodcutters, blacksmiths and porters.

It is not only by giving of one's wealth that one can be kind to others. A cheerful word, an encouraging smile, a friendly handshake, all help in promoting peace, harmony and love among men. Of a Rabbi it is said that he never failed to greet others before they greeted him and this was true even if they were idolaters. When a man goes to Heaven, the Rabbis taught, the first question he is asked by God is whether he was honest in his dealings with his fellow-men.

The Sabbath

Jews rest from work on the seventh day of the week. The book of Genesis, the first book in the Bible, tells how God created the world in six days and rested on the seventh. Of course this is really a piece of poetry. God cannot be worn out after His labours that He should need to rest. What it really means, as Judaism understands it, is that by man finishing his work before the Sabbath and finding on it rest and refreshment, he acknowledges God as the Creator of the world.

The sabbath is described as a day of delight. It is a religious duty to eat well of tasty foods on this day. The

The family sit around a festive table

family sit around a festive table and sing pleasant songs in which all join in. The Sabbath begins on Friday night and ends at nightfall on Saturday. Before the Friday night meal, the father of the house pours some wine into a silver goblet and thanks God for His goodness, referring to God's creation of the world. All present drink a little of the wine. Wine drinking is not held to be in any way sinful in Judaism. On the contrary, it is a religious obligation to drink wine on the Sabbaths and the festivals, though drunkenness is severely frowned upon. The Sabbath is the day more than others when Jews go to the synagogue. The Rabbis have a beautiful saying that the person who keeps the Sabbath acquires for the day an extra soul.

Passover

The Jewish year is made colourful by a number of festivals, each with its own message. One of the most important of these is Passover. On this festival Jews celebrate the deliverance of their people from Egyptian slavery. Another name for the festival is, therefore, the feast of freedom. The highlight of the festival is the home ceremony on the first night. On this occasion the old tale is retold of how God saved the Israelites from Egypt. Each member of the family drinks no fewer than four cups of wine (very small ones for the children) because in the story as told in the Biblical book of Exodus four different words are used to describe God's deliverance. We are also told there that the people were in such a hurry to get away from Egypt that they had no time to bake their bread properly and so had to eat "unleavened bread", that is, bread that has had no time to rise. On Passover, flat cakes of delicious unleavened bread are eaten and no ordinary bread is kept in the house. Among other dishes eaten at the meal on the first night are bitter herbs (a reminder of the bitterness of slavery) and a mixture of apples, almonds and wine (a paste-like dish, a reminder of the mortar used by the slaves as they toiled).

The children are the heroes of this evening. There

The children search for unleavened bread

are a number of tuneful songs with comical words arranged especially for the children to sing. The youngest child at the table asks the father four questions about why the night of Passover is different from all other nights and the father replies that it is because God saved the Israelites. A portion of unleavened bread is hidden by the father at the beginning of the celebration. The child lucky enough to find it is rewarded with a present.

Tabernacles

Tabernacles is an autumn festival while Passover is a spring festival. On Tabernacles Jews, if they possibly can, have their meals in a "hut" or "tabernacle" which they build before the festival. This is a reminder of the tents in which the Israelites dwelled as they journeyed through the desert for forty years until they reached Palestine. (You see how in the festivals the Jewish past is brought back to life.) The tabernacle is a simple hut open to the sky but lightly covered with fragrant leaves and boughs of trees. The hut is decorated with fruit of all kinds hanging from the leafy roof. On this festival palm branches, citrons (a kind of lemon) as well as willows and myrtles are paraded around the synagogue. In ancient times this was the harvest festival at the end of the harvest when thanks were given to God for causing the crops, trees and flowers to grow.

The end of the harvest

The New Year

The Jewish New Year begins in September or October. The year 1972, for instance, is in the Jewish calendar 5732 (counted from "the creation of the world", though most Jews nowadays accept the scientific view that the world is, in fact, much older). The New Year festival is a more serious occasion than other festivals. At the beginning of the year the Jew takes stock of his life and makes up his mind to lead a better life in the year ahead. The synagogues are crowded on New Year's

31

BBC Hulton Picture Library
A ram's horn is blown during the festival

day. During the synagogue service a ram's horn (the oldest musical instrument known to man) is blown. The ram's horn produces sharp, piercing notes that sound rather like weeping. This is to remind the people to weep for their mistakes in the past year and to wake up (rather like an alarm clock) to a better life in the coming year.

The Day of Atonement

Ten days after the New Year festival there falls the great fast of the Day of Atonement. Adults (but not children) eat no food and take no drinks for 24 hours, spending the greater part of the day in the synagogue. During the services of the day there are long confessions of sin because "atonement" really means "forgiveness" and God forgives the sins of those who are truly sorry. But although the day is one of great solemnity it is at the same time a partly joyous occasion since it is the time when men make their peace with God. Some people who see it only from the outside call this day

The scapegoat: Leviticus 16:22

"the black fast" but this is nonsense. Jews refer to it as the "white fast", white being the symbol of cleanliness and purity. Some of the more pious folk wear

33

white robes on this day over their ordinary clothes. On this day the service is chanted to ancient melodies some of which are said to go back to the songs the priests sang in the Temple.

Chanukkah

This is a winter festival and it means "dedication" of the Temple. Over 2,000 years ago a certain King Antiochus wanted to force the Jews to give up their religion. The Jews, though few in numbers compared with the armies of the tyrant, fought back and succeeded in recapturing the Temple. Now in the Temple oil lamps were kindled in a candelabra but after the victory there could only be found enough oil for one night. Legend tells how the oil continued to burn by a miracle for eight nights until fresh oil could be obtained. This has been understood to mean that the light of the spirit burns miraculously even against very heavy odds. Consequently, on this festival candles are placed in a candelabra (every Jewish home has one of these specially for the festival). One candle is added each night until, on the eighth night, the whole candelabra is ablaze with light. Presents are given to the children, games are played, and there is general jollification all round.

34

The Dietary Laws

You may have heard that Jews do not eat pork. Nor do they eat birds of prey. No one knows of the precise reason for these and other restrictions on diet but a number of suggestions have been made. The pig, for example, is not exactly a clean animal and birds of prey are symbols of cruelty. There are many laws of this kind in Judaism. There are three different attitudes towards them among Jews of today. Orthodox Jews still try their best to keep all the laws. Reform Jews believe that it is up to the individual whether or not he keeps them but that, in any case, the really important laws are not these but those about good conduct towards one's fellows. Conservative Jews have a middle attitude. They try to keep all the laws but not as strictly as do the Orthodox. Similarly, in the services of the synagogue. Orthodox Jews will be more in favour than Reform Jews of retaining all the old prayers and of using only Hebrew in prayer.

Birth

There is great rejoicing in a Jewish home whenever a child is born. From the time of the Bible children are

35

A special prayer is recited in the synagogue for a new infant

considered to be a blessing. A new human being has come into the world and the hope is expressed that the child will grow up to be a faithful and loyal Jew, carrying on the traditions of the Jewish people. Judaism teaches that to marry and have children is a religious duty. That is why, for instance, very few Rabbis remain unmarried.

After the birth of a child the proud father attends the synagogue and he is called to the reading of the Torah from the scroll. A special prayer is recited for the new infant to grow up to be strong, healthy and firm in attachment to the Jewish faith.

Bar Mitzvah

A little child cannot be expected to have a proper sense of responsibility. Therefore, Judaism teaches, God's commands are not addressed to children (although their parents are expected to train them in the way of Judaism) but to adults. When does a child become an "adult" for this purpose? The answer of the ancient Rabbis is that a boy becomes a fully responsible Jew at the age of thirteen. He is then *Bar* ("son of") *Mitzvah* ("the command"). The Rabbis believed that girls are more intelligent than boys (do you agree?) so that a girl becomes *Bat* ("daughter of") *Mitzvah* at the age of twelve. On reaching this age boys (in some communities girls as well) take part in a special ceremony to mark the occasion.

On the Sabbath after his thirteenth birthday the Bar Mitzvah attends the synagogue together with his parents and other relatives where he chants aloud a portion from the scroll and another portion from one of the books of the prophets. He has to recite these in Hebrew and there is a special tune for the reading from the scroll and a different tune for the reading from the prophets. So you can imagine that he has to spend considerable time beforehand to make himself familiar with it all if he wishes to carry out his task well. After he has read his portions the Rabbi of the congregation addresses him in public to remind him of his new responsibilities as a fully-fledged Jew. His parents, pleased that their son has reached this important milestone in his life, hold a party to which they invite their friends. The boy is generally called upon to make a speech in which he thanks his parents for all they have done for him and thanks the guests for the presents they have sent him (most Bar Mitzvah boys find

On his thirteenth birthday a Jewish boy is given a party

themselves with a surfeit of fountain pens after the event and there is a Jewish story about the Bar Mitzvah boy who began his speech with: "Today I am a fountain pen"). He also states his resolve to live up to the best traditions of Judaism.

Marriage

One of the most interesting Jewish ceremonies is the wedding ceremony. The bride and bridegroom stand under a special canopy which represents the home in which they are about to live together. The canopy is often decorated with flowers. During the ceremony their parents stand by their side. The Rabbi takes a cup of wine and he recites a blessing in which he thanks God for the institution of marriage. He then hands the wine to the parents who in turn hand it to the bride and bridegroom who take a sip of the wine. The bridegroom then places the ring on the forefinger of the bride's right hand. (On the right hand and not on the left because in Hebrew and in other languages "right" is the symbol of all the good things.) When he gives the ring to the bride the bridegroom says: "Behold thou art consecrated unto me with this ring according to the law of Moses and of Israel". The Rabbi then takes a second cup of wine and recites seven further blessings in which he asks God to pour out his goodness on the young couple and make them very happy in their future. Again he hands the wine to the parents who hand it to the bride and bridegroom.

One of the seven blessings recited under the canopy reads: "Blessed art Thou, O Lord our God, King of

A Jewish wedding ceremony

the universe, who hast created joy and gladness, bride-groom and bride, mirth and exultation, pleasure and delight, love, brotherhood, peace and fellowship. Soon, O Lord our God, may there be heard in the cities of Judah, and in the streets of Jerusalem, the voice of joy and gladness, the voice of the bridegroom and the voice of the bride, the jubilant voice of bridegrooms from their canopies, and of youths from their feasts of song. Blessed art Thou, O Lord, who makest the bridegroom rejoice with the bride".

At the end of the ceremony the bridegroom stamps on a glass and breaks it. Various reasons have been given for this strange custom. One of them is that it is a reminder of the destruction of the Temple, that is to say, to remind the bride and bridegroom that there are, unfortunately, people who do harm in the world but that they should build a home in which there is love for one another and love for their fellow-men.

Death

When a person dies the body is washed and then dressed in clean, white linen shrouds. To prepare the body for burial in this way is held to be a high honour and in many Jewish communities is carried out by the most respected members of the community. The body is then placed in a simple coffin of plain wood. At the

41

burial the nearest relatives and the other people present shovel a little earth into the grave. Many Jews observe the mourning customs. For seven days after the burial they remain at home and sit on low stools. Prayers for the soul of the departed are recited by visitors to the house of mourning. It is considered to be a strong religious duty to visit mourners and offer them words of comfort in their sorrow.

A Jewish burial

For eleven months after the death of a parent a son attends synagogue services during which he recites aloud a prayer known as the Kaddish. The word means "holiness" or "sanctity" and the prayer is so called because in it the son prays for God's holiness to be felt by all men. The Kaddish prayer begins: "Magnified and sanctified be His great name in the world which He hath created according to His will. May He establish His kingdom during your life and during your days, and during the life of all the house of Israel, even speedily and at a near time, and say ye, Amen". The meaning of it is that the parent in Heaven is pleased that he has left behind him a son who follows his religion. This prayer is also recited by the son each year on the anniversary of the death of his parents. On the anniversary of a death in the family the members of the family keep a light burning for the whole of the day because in the Bible man's soul is compared to a light kindled by God.

Blessings

We have referred to blessings recited at the wedding ceremony. In addition, Judaism knows of many such blessings in which man thanks God for His goodness. The good Jew is encouraged to recite a blessing before eating and drinking and when he admires God's wonderful world. The idea behind it all is that life is good and man should appreciate God's gifts and give thanks to Him for them. Here are a few of these blessings:

To be recited before eating meat or fish or cheese:

"Blessed art Thou, O Lord our God, King of the universe, by whose word all things exist".

To be recited before smelling fragrant spices:

"Blessed art Thou, O Lord our God, King of the universe, who createst different kinds of spices".

To be recited before eating bread:

"Blessed art Thou, O Lord our God, King of the universe, who bringeth forth bread from the earth".

To be recited before eating fruit:

"Blessed art Thou, O Lord our God, King of the universe, who createst the fruit of the tree".

To be recited before eating vegetables:

"Blessed art Thou, O Lord our God, King of the universe, who createst the fruit of the earth".

To be recited before drinking wine:

"Blessed art Thou, O Lord our God, King of the universe, who createst the fruit of the vine".

On hearing thunder:

"Blessed art Thou, O Lord our God, King of the universe, whose strength and might fill the world".

On seeing lightning, or falling stars or high mountains:

"Blessed art Thou, O Lord our God, King of the universe, who hast made the creation".

On seeing beautiful trees or animals:

"Blessed art Thou, O Lord our God, King of the universe, who hast such as these in Thy world".

On seeing a wise man:

"Blessed art Thou, O Lord our God, King of the universe, who hast given of Thy wisdom to flesh and blood".

On seeing a king:

"Blessed art Thou, O Lord our God, King of the universe, who hast given of Thy glory to flesh and blood".

On seeing giants or dwarfs:

"Blessed art Thou, O Lord our God, King of the universe, who variest the forms of Thy creatures".

The People of the Book

Mohammed called the Jews "the people of the book". It is true that the Jewish people have loved books, especially the books of the Bible. Strictly speaking, the Bible is not one single book. It is really a collection of books, written over a very long period. The earlier books of the Bible were written hundreds of years before the latest books. The Jewish tradition knows of twenty-four books of the Bible. These are divided into three sections: 1) Torah; 2) Prophets; 3) Writings.

Jewish people have loved books

Torah

As we have seen, the word Torah ("teaching") means the whole of Judaism. But in its more detailed sense the word refers to the first five books of the Bible: The Five Books of Moses. These are: Genesis, Exodus, Leviticus, Numbers and Deuteronomy. Genesis deals with the creation of the world; the early history of mankind; and the lives of Abraham, Isaac and Jacob. Exodus deals with the deliverance of the Israelites from the slavery of Egypt and the march of the slaves towards the land they had been promised. Leviticus deals with the laws of sacrifices in the sanctuary. Numbers continues with the story of how the people, after they had left Egypt, journeyed for forty years through the wilderness. Deuteronomy describes the farewell speeches Moses made to the people before he died. Moses died in the land of Moab at the threshold of the promised land.

Prophets

This section of the Bible contains a number of historical books as well as the actual books of the prophets. There is a tradition that these books were, in fact, written by the prophets. The books in this section of the Bible are, in the order in which they occur: Joshua, Judges, Samuel, Kings, Isaiah, Jeremiah, Ezekiel, the book of the Twelve Prophets. The books of Joshua, Judges, Samuel and Kings continue to describe the early history of the people. Joshua was the leader after Moses. After Joshua's death there arose a series of men (and one woman, Deborah), who led the people. These were called "Judges", which, in this context, means people gifted with qualities of leadership. The book of Samuel tells of how Saul and later David were appointed as the kings of the people and the book of Kings takes up the story with the kings who came after David. You might think it a little odd that there should be so much history in the Bible. The answer is that the ancient Israelites believed very strongly that God guides men through their history and that, therefore, there is something "religious" about it all.

The books of Isaiah, Jeremiah and Ezekiel contain the teachings of these three great prophets. The book of the twelve contains the teachings of: Hosea, Joel, Amos, Obadiah, Jonah, Micah, Nahum, Habakkuk, Zephaniah, Haggai, Zechariah and Malachi. The reason why these twelve were all put into a single book is that, compared with Isaiah, Jeremiah and Ezekiel, these books are so small in size. Obadiah, for instance, has only one chapter. Little books could easily be lost so they were put together in one large book. That is why these twelve are sometimes called "minor prophets". This does not mean that they are of minor importance but that their books are small in size.

The books of the Bible were written by the prophets   49

Writings

The third division of the Bible is a series of writings which were considered to be holy or sacred (and are, therefore, part of the Bible) but not to the same extent as the books of the prophets. These writings are: Psalms, Proverbs, Job, Song of Songs, Ruth, Lamentations, Ecclesiastes, Esther, Daniel, Ezra, Nehemiah, Chronicles. The book of Psalms contains some of the most magnificent religious poetry ever written. It has been used in worship not only by Jews but by religious people all over the world. The book of Proverbs contains a good deal of sound advice on how life should be lived. It was produced in the circles of the "wise men" of ancient Israel. Job tells of a very good man who suffered greatly and it raises the question of why God, who is good, should allow men to suffer. The Song of Songs is a collection of beautiful love poems. Ruth tells of a gentle woman from the land of Moab who became the ancestress of King David. Lamentations is a series of dirges written after the destruction of the Temple. Ecclesiastes is the book of a sceptic who was puzzled by the injustices he saw all around him. Esther tells the story of the Jewish girl who became the Queen of Persia and who helped to save her people from destruction. Daniel tells of a hero who was so loyal to his

Daniel in the lions' den

religion that he was prepared to be thrown into a lions' den rather than be false to it. Ezra and Nehemiah tell of the deeds of these two leaders who established the Jewish state once again after the people had been driven into exile in Babylon. The book of Chronicles is another history book, taking the story down to the end of the Biblical period.

These twenty-four books became the Hebrew Bible. There was a saying in ancient times that a bride wore twenty-four different ornaments on the day of her wedding and the people of Israel are, similarly, adorned

51

by the twenty-four books of the Bible. Of the three divisions of the Bible the Torah is held to be the most sacred, next the Prophets and thirdly the Writings. Even today some pious Jews will never place a book of the Writings on top of a book of the Prophets or a book of the Prophets on top of a copy of the Torah. If one of these books falls to the ground the pious Jew will lift it up with reverence and kiss it.

The pious Jew will lift up the book and kiss it should it fall to the ground

The Talmud

Study of books did not stop with the Bible. For many centuries after the Bible had been completed the Jewish teachers, later called the Rabbis, continued to discuss the earlier teachings and add to them many of their own. Over fifteen hundred years ago all these teachings and ideas were gathered together in the gigantic work known as the Talmud. In the printed editions of the Talmud there are no less than thirty-two huge volumes containing about five million words! The word "Talmud", you will not be surprised to learn, is another word meaning "teaching".

There are discussions in the Talmud of almost every subject under the sun. Some of the topics dealt with at length are: law, ethics, history, geography, astronomy, folk-lore and superstitions, medicine, wise sayings, popular proverbs, wit and humour, detective stories and other tales, Greek, Roman and Persian civilisation, biology and mathematics. The Talmud has fed numerous Jewish minds over the ages. Some Jewish scholars have devoted their whole lives to mastering its contents. Only the keenest minds have been capable of this feat.

What Jews Believe

Eight hundred years ago there lived in Egypt a great Jewish doctor, teacher and thinker by the name of Maimonides. He drew up a list of thirteen principles of the Jewish faith, thirteen things in which a Jew is expected to believe. Not all Jewish thinkers agreed with Maimonides and even those who did sometimes went their own way in interpreting these beliefs. But, on the whole, the list prepared by Maimonides does give us a good idea of what Jews believe. Here are the thirteen principles.

Maimonides

The first principle is that God exists. Without a belief in God there can be no Judaism.

The second principle is that there is only one God and that belief in any other gods is false. This is called monotheism, which means belief in one God. Included in this belief is the further one that God is the Creator of the whole world.

The third principle is that God has no body. If God had a body He would not be God at all. God is a Spirit. Although we frequently think of God as a kind of old man in the sky this principle says that we must never imagine that He is really like that. We have to use pictures when we think of Him but we must not think of the picture as really describing God.

The fourth principle is that God is eternal. This means that God was not born, nor can He die, but He lives for ever and ever and has always lived.

The fifth principle is that one should only pray to God and not offer prayers to any other being. Jews never pray to angels, for example, or to holy men, only to God Himself.

The sixth principle is that the words of the prophets are true, that the teachings of the prophets as found in the Bible are sound teachings which men do well to heed.

The seventh principle is that Moses was the greatest of the prophets. Although, as we have seen, in Judaism the centre of the stage is occupied by the Jewish people,

55

not by any particular great man, yet there have been great Jewish individuals, and of these Moses was the greatest. The most important teachings about how men should live are to be found in the Five Books of Moses.

The eighth principle is that the teachings of Moses were given to him by God Himself. This principle means that the Torah was revealed to Moses by God. How God gave the Torah to men is a mystery beyond our understanding. But it is not the *how* which matters but the fact that God did so.

The ninth principle is that the Torah is God's final word and that He has never revealed nor will He ever again reveal another Torah. This principle means that Judaism does not agree with Christianity and Islam, both of which say that God did once reveal Himself to Israel but later made a new revelation, to Jesus or to Mohammed. Judaism says that God does not change His mind.

The tenth principle is that God knows everything there is to know and this includes all the deeds of men and all their thoughts. A man may plot to do harm to others thinking that no one will ever know. But God knows.

The eleventh principle is that God rewards those who do good and punishes those who do evil. God wants men to lead good lives. If they do He will see to it that they are made happy. If they do not He will see to it that they are made miserable. But this does not

Moses

mean that a man should always think in terms of reward. The Rabbis say that the good man will do good simply because it is right so to do and he will leave the rest to God.

The twelfth principle is that the Messiah will come. The Messiah (the word means an anointed king) is a person who will be sent by God to lead all men to live far better lives and to establish a new kind of society. Some Jews believe in the Messiah as an actual person to be sent in the future by God. Others think rather of the age of the Messiah, that is of a more perfect society in the future in which all men will come to know the truth. What it all means is that Judaism is sufficiently optimistic to believe that one day all the things that make life so bitter — hatred and war and poverty and so forth — will be banished from earth and all men will know God.

The thirteenth principle is that the dead will rise again. This means that Judaism does not believe that when a man dies that is the end of him. The soul of man lives for ever.

The Jew and the World

While it is true that Judaism speaks in the first instance
to the Jewish people, this does not mean that Judaism
has no interest in mankind as a whole. That would be
absurd since Jews believe that God is the Father of all
men who are His children whom He loves. That is why
the Rabbis say that every man, Jew or non-Jew, if he
leads a decent, good life, will go to Heaven when he
dies. And that is why one of the prophets, speaking of
the Messianic age, said: "And the Lord shall be King
over all the earth. On that day the Lord shall be One
and His name One".

God is the Father of all men

Index